FROM FARM TO YOU

Honey

Carol Jones

CHELSEA HOUSE
PUBLISHERS

A Haights Cross Communications Company

Philadelphia

This edition first published in 2003 in the United States of America by Chelsea House Publishers, a subsidiary of Haights Cross Communications.

Chelsea House Publishers
1974 Sproul Road, Suite 400
Broomall, PA 19008-0914

The Chelsea House world wide web address is www.chelseahouse.com

Library of Congress Cataloging-in-Publication Data Applied for.
ISBN 0-7910-7009-3

First published in 2002 by
MACMILLAN EDUCATION AUSTRALIA PTY LTD
627 Chapel Street, South Yarra, Australia, 3141

Edited by Anne McKenna
Text design by Judith Summerfeldt Grace
Cover design by Judith Summerfeldt Grace
Illustration on p. 23 by Pat Kermode, Purple Rabbit Productions

Printed in China

Acknowledgements
The author wishes to thank Brian Tanis of Ambrosia Apiaries for his help with the writing of this book.

Cover photographs: Jar of honey courtesy of Corbis, honeycomb courtesy of Getty Images/Photodisc.

APL/Corbis © Lynda Richardson, p. 4, © Christie's Images, p. 5, © Frank Lane Picture Agency, p. 10 (bottom right), © Owen Franken, p. 27, © Gail Mooney, p. 28 (France); Artville, pp. 3 (top right), 29 (USA); Capilano Honey, p. 25 (bottom); Coo-ee Picture Library, p. 9 (bottom); Copper Leife/Craig Forsythe, pp. 8 (bottom), 12 (top), 28 (Lebanon), 29 (Australia); Pavel German/Nature Focus, p. 10 (bottom left); Getty Images/Photodisc, pp. 3 (top left), 7 (top), 8–9 (top), 13, 28 (Belgium and Denmark), pp. 28–29 (map), 29 (China); Carol Jones, pp. 3 (bottom left and right), 14–19; Peter Kaczynski, pp. 10–11, 12 (bottom), 22, 25 (top); Mary Evans Picture Library, pp. 6 (bottom), 7 (bottom); Photolibrary.com/FoodPix, p. 28 (Italy); SkyScans/David Hancock, p. 6 (top); Ken Stepnell, pp. 20–1.

Contents

The world of honey

Honey is a natural food collected from beehives. It needs no other ingredients added to it, and it requires very little **processing**.

Single-flower honeys are made by bees that gather **nectar** from one kind of flower. There are also blended honeys made by bees in different places gathering nectar from different kinds of plants.

People who live in warm and **temperate** climates around the world have been raiding beehives since before recorded history. Honey does not need **preservatives** to keep it fresh. It can be eaten straight from the honeycomb, and it is a natural sweetener.

Honey is a sweet treat that can be eaten on its own.

The history of honey

Honey is an ancient food. Honey and bees have been featured in many myths and legends from around the world.

The Cheyenne people of North America have a creation myth that tells of the first people living on honey and wild fruits.

Bees are native to many countries, and early peoples braved angry bees to collect honey. A 12,000-year-old rock painting in a cave in Spain shows a man putting his hand into a hole to collect honey while holding a basket with his other hand.

Ancient Egyptians collected honey by smoking bees from their nests. As well as eating the honey, they used it as a medicine. They also left honeycomb to **ferment** in water, making an alcoholic drink we call mead. Far away on the Amazon River in South America, people also discovered how to make mead.

In some cultures honey was used as a medicine.

Firsts

The ancient Egyptians were the first to breed bees. One 2,700-year-old tomb painting in Thebes shows pottery hives shaped like wine jars. They also used honey to **embalm** mummies.

Both the ancient Greeks and Romans used honey in cooking savory and sweet dishes. Honey was used to make sauces and stuffings for meat, as well as puddings and cakes. The Roman army in France and Greece sometimes kept beehives as a hobby.

One early method of setting up a beehive was to collect the nests of wild bees. For example, if the bees nested in a hollow in the trunk or branch of a tree, someone might chop down the tree or branch and take it home. Later beekeepers made hives of burnt-out tree trunks and woven baskets.

In Australia, Aboriginal people have collected honey or 'sugarbag' from native beehives for centuries. They also used this honey as an ointment.

Strange but true!

The ancient Greek philosopher Democritus lived very cheaply. At the age of 109 he decided to leave one more food out of his diet every day until there was nothing left. But since he did not want to die during the important religious festival of Demeter, he had a pot of honey brought to him. Once the festival was over, the philosopher put away the honey to die peacefully.

A pyramid-shaped beehive from about 1840

In the **Middle Ages**, honey was the most commonly used sweetener. It is mentioned in *The Tales of a Thousand and One Nights* from the **Middle East**. The monks of England kept bees for their honey and to collect beeswax for making candles. The Vikings of Denmark kept bees to make mead, which they drank from metal drinking horns.

Bees have been kept in hives made from wooden tubs, casks and frames, plaited wicker and pottery for nearly 3,000 years. However, little was known about the bees themselves until the end of the 1600s when Dutch doctor Jan Swammerdam discovered that the 'king' or father of bees was really a queen!

Spiced honey cakes are often shaped into houses or people. The most famous is the witch's gingerbread house in the fairytale *Hansel and Gretel*.

Making beeswax candles in the 1800s

Famous honey breads

The cake we call gingerbread or spice-bread has a famous past. In China 1,000 years ago, people enjoyed honey bread made from wheat flour and honey. The horsemen of Ghengis Khan carried honey bread in their saddlebags as they conquered much of Central Asia and Eastern Europe. The pastry cooks of France had many famous recipes for spice-bread. To become a Master Spice-bread Maker in France in the 1500s, a cook had to bake three huge honey cakes weighing 9 pounds (20 kilograms) each!

Kinds of honey

Honey gets its flavor from the flowers the bees visit. Each type of flower gives the honey a different flavor. Honey can also be packed in different ways.

1. Single-flower honey

Beekeepers place groups of hives in different places, called bee sites. The flavor, color and thickness of honey from each site depends on the kind of flowering plant in the area. Honeys vary in color from nearly white to very dark brown. In the United States there are even purple, red and green honeys. In Australia two of the most tasty single-flower honeys are leatherwood and yellow box.

2. Blended honey

Honey packers can mix honey collected from many bee sites. This makes blended honeys cheaper to produce than single-flower honeys. Most of the honey produced in factories is blended liquid honey.

Honey comes in many different colors, flavors and thicknesses.

Honey can be eaten straight from the honeycomb.

3. Candied and creamed honey

As well as liquid honey, honey packers sell candied and creamed honey. Some types of honey 'candy', or form crystals, very quickly. Creamed honey is a thick creamy paste made by whipping candied honey with liquid honey.

4. Comb honey

Instead of removing the honey from the honeycomb, sometimes beekeepers cut the honeycomb into sections with the honey inside. The honey fills your mouth when you chew on the honeycomb.

These beekeepers are removing honeycomb from a hive.

Preservation

Honey has long been used as a preservative. The Romans preserved fruits and vegetables in honey. For example, turnips were preserved in a mixture of honey and vinegar. In India, meat was preserved for the next year in honey. Even bodies have been preserved in honey. When Alexander the Great (conqueror of most of Europe) died in 323 B.C., his body was embalmed in honey.

The bees

Honey bees are **social** insects that live and work together in a **colony**. They gather nectar from flowers to make honey to feed the colony.

There are 20,000 different kinds of bees in the world. One species, the honey bee, produces so much honey that there is enough to feed the entire bee colony, with enough left for people to collect.

Honey bees have been bred by humans for centuries. There are three honey bee **races** that are often kept by beekeepers. Italian bees have brightly colored bodies. Gray-haired Caucasian bees are native to Russia. They can live in colder weather. Carniolan bees come from Austria. They are dark colored with gray hairs.

A honey bee on a flower

Worker bees feeding larvae in honeycomb cells

Italian honey bees like these prefer warmer weather.

A bee chewing out of its cocoon

Bee castes

In every honey bee colony there are three **castes** of bees: the queen, the male drones, and the female workers.

The queen lays the eggs in honeycomb cells. Queens live for up to four years, but beekeepers usually replace them every year as they lay the most eggs in their first year. The male drones mate with the new queen when she makes her mating flight. As soon as they have mated, the drones die.

The female workers have many jobs during their six weeks of life. They feed the other bees and **larvae**. They store the nectar and build the honeycomb. They guard the hive and **ripen** the honey. And they forage, or search, for nectar, pollen and water.

Bee larvae

Eggs hatch into larvae inside honeycomb cells. When the larvae are grown, worker bees close the honeycomb cells. Like butterfly larvae, bee larvae spin cocoons around themselves and gradually change into worker, drone or queen bees. Then they chew their way out of the cocoons.

Making the honey

Worker bees gather nectar and carry it back to the hive where it is ripened into honey.

Each morning, worker bees scout for flowers that produce a lot of nectar, called honey flora. The scouts use a special dance to tell other foragers where to find the honey flora. The foragers suck the nectar from the flowers with their **proboscis** and store it in pouches inside their bodies, called honey sacs. They also collect **pollen** to eat. The flower pollen rubs off onto their body hair. They comb the pollen from their hair with their legs or antennae and store it on their back legs.

Foragers suck the nectar from flowers.

Pollen is stored on the bees' back legs.

Conservation

Most flowering plants need to be pollinated to grow seeds. Many plants pollinate themselves but as bees travel from flower to flower pollen sticks to the hairs on their bodies. The pollen then rubs off on another flower and can pollinate it. In this way, bees can cross-pollinate one plant with another of the same species. This makes plants stronger.

Back at the hive, foragers pass the nectar to other worker bees' mouths. **Enzymes** in the bees' mouths will help turn the nectar into honey.

The nectar is placed into honeycomb cells. (Other cells have been chosen as brood cells for raising larvae.) The enzymes cause the sugars in the nectar, called sucrose, to change into honey sugars, called glucose, fructose and maltose. To get rid of extra moisture in the ripening honey, workers move their muscles to create heat and fan their wings to move more air around.

When the honey is ready, workers close off the cells with beeswax to stop moisture or air getting in and spoiling the honey.

Honey is ripened in honeycomb cells.

How honey is collected

A person who looks after bees is called a beekeeper. Beekeepers usually manage as many as 1,000 hives.

Beekeepers process the honey and may deliver it to a honey packing company. The beekeeper shown here collects and packs his own honey.

Tools and equipment

Beekeepers use many different tools to do their work. One of the most important is the hive. Each hive is a specially made wooden box with several compartments. Beekeepers need to wear protective clothing so they do not get stung by the bees. A smoker is needed to remove the honey. A forklift and truck are used to transport hives to bee sites and drums of honey to the honey packing company.

The beekeeper uses machines such as an uncapping machine, an extractor, a spinner and a settling tank to process the honey.

The beekeeper is working at a bee site

Drums of honey

14

Preparing to collect the honey

The beekeeper visits one of the sites where he keeps beehives. First he lights the smoker. The smoker is a can with a **bellows** attached. It burns fuel such as bark, twigs or pine needles. The beekeeper uses the bellows to pump air over the smoldering fuel to make a cool smoke. The smoke confuses the bees' defense signals and they become calm. This allows the beekeeper to remove the frames of honey from the hive more easily.

Then the beekeeper puts on protective clothing: overalls, long gloves, and a bee hat with a veil. Despite this clothing, beekeepers can still be stung while collecting honey.

A beehive

The smoker

Beekeepers wear special clothing to protect them from bee stings.

Removing the frames

The beekeeper places the smoker at the hive entrance to calm the bees. Then he lifts the lid from the hive. The hive is made from several boxes called honey **supers** stacked on top of each other. The bees are still restless so he uses the smoker again, then pulls out a frame. Each frame is a wooden rectangle with thin wires strung across. Each super contains several frames. The bees build their honeycomb inside the frame then fill it with honey. Then they cap the honey-filled cells with beeswax.

The beekeeper gently taps the frame to remove the bees. He removes frames full of honey and replaces them with empty frames for the bees to build more honeycomb and fill it with honey. Some beekeepers find it quicker to blow off the bees with a garden blower and remove the whole honey super.

Removing a frame filled with honey and covered with bees

Uncapping the honey

The beekeeper transports the frames to his small factory nearby. Each full frame weighs about 5 to 7 pounds (2 to 3 kilograms). The beeswax must be removed to get the honey from the honeycomb inside. Some beekeepers use a hot knife to cut the wax from both sides of the frame. This beekeeper puts the frames into an uncapping machine. Very sharp mechanical knives move backwards and forwards cutting off the wax.

The wax caps can be melted down and sold as beeswax. Beeswax is used to make candles, furniture polish and lipstick.

The beekeeper places the full frames into an uncapping machine.

The uncapping machine cuts the wax from the frame of honey.

Extracting the honey

The beekeeper slides the uncapped frames into an extractor. An extractor looks like a large round tank with wire slots to hold the frames. The frames are spun around inside the tank. Extractors can hold from 24 to 120 frames, depending on their size.

Inside the tank, the extractor spins so fast that the honey is forced out of the honeycomb. The honey runs down the sides of the extractor, then flows into a trough at the bottom.

Frames are placed in an extractor and spun around to remove the honey.

Spinning and settling the honey

Honey is pumped into a spinner to remove any remaining pieces of wax, honeycomb and **crystallized** honey. The liquid honey runs into a settling tank. Most beekeepers then fill large steel drums with honey for transport to a honey packer. This beekeeper packs his own honey.

A spinner removes any remaining wax from the honey.

Bottling and labeling the honey

The beekeeper places a label on each bottle with a small labeling machine. The bottle is then placed under an air-driven bottling machine that fills the bottle with honey. The lids are screwed on by hand.

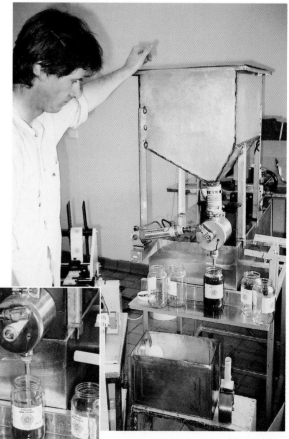

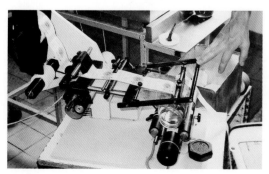
Labeling the honey

Bottling the honey

The honey factory

Honey is a natural food made by bees in beehives and collected by beekeepers. Most of the honey we buy is packaged in large factories.

From nature to consumer

Follow the flowchart to see how honey is collected, processed in large factories and then transported to stores for sale to the **consumer**.

Read more about each stage of honey making and processing and how honey is marketed and sold on pages 22 to 27. Look for the flowchart symbols that represent each stage of the process.

Collecting the honey
Bees make honey by gathering nectar from flowers. Beekeepers keep bees in beehives and collect their honey.

Packaging the honey
Packaging materials may be made elsewhere and delivered to the honey packer. Honey packing companies do the final processing and packaging.

Transport and storage
The packaged honey is transported by truck to stores or to ports.

Transport and storage
Beekeepers use a forklift and truck to transport hives to bee sites. They use the truck to take frames of honeycomb to their small factories for processing.

Transport and storage
Honey is stored in drums and transported by forklift and truck to the honey packer.

Processing the honey

Beekeepers remove the honey from the honeycomb and send it to a large honey packer for further processing.

Marketing and selling honey

Honey is sold locally in supermarkets and food stores. Honey is also exported for sale in other countries.

Buying honey

The consumer buys honey from the supermarket or food store. It will keep almost indefinitely in an airtight container.

Collecting the honey

In the wild, honey bees make nests in trees and gather nectar to make honey. Beekeepers keep honey bees in specially made wooden beehives and collect the honey made by the bees. Each hive can hold up to 100,000 bees! A group of hives on one site is called an apiary.

Beekeepers choose bee sites carefully. They need plenty of flowering plants and water so the bees can cool their hives in hot weather. Most bee sites are located on farms or near forests with flowering trees. Beekeepers know which plants have the most pollen and nectar for making honey.

Beekeepers use a forklift to load hives onto trucks.

Transport and storage

Beekeepers move their hives using forklifts to lift the hives onto their trucks. The collected honey is stored in a settling tank before being pumped into large metal drums and transported by truck to the honey packer.

During winter, beekeepers mend their equipment, paint the hives and check that bees are healthy and have enough food. In spring they continue to check water and food supplies and ensure the queens are laying eggs to keep up the hive population. They also start collecting honey. Summer is when most honey is collected. Sometimes beekeepers start new colonies by taking several frames full of bees and putting them into a new hive with a new queen.

Beekeepers wear protective clothing when they remove frames of honey from the hives. Then they slice the wax caps off the honeycomb and remove the honey before shipping it to a honey packer in large drums.

lid

hole to allow air to move around

frames inside honey super

the frames with the queen and brood cells (eggs) are separated from the frames with honey cells by the queen excluder

frames inside a brood chamber where the queen lives

bottom board with space for bees to enter and leave the beehive

A typical wooden beehive

Honey workers

Beekeepers

Bees

Strange but true!

It takes 500 honey bees four weeks to collect enough nectar to make about 2 pounds (1 kilogram) of honey.

Processing the honey

Honey packers sample each drum delivered by beekeepers to check color and moisture content. Honey with too much moisture cannot be used. Honey tasters taste the honey to make sure single-flower honeys taste true.

The drums are heated to 83 degrees Fahrenheit (45 degrees Celsius) to make honey easier to pour. The honey is then poured into pit tanks below the ground. There the honey settles for 12 hours so that beeswax will float to the top.

Honey is pumped through a filter to remove beeswax and bits of plant matter. It then passes through a water-heated heat exchanger to reheat the honey. From there a clarifier spins the honey very fast, removing more beeswax. And just in case any plant matter remains, the honey is pumped through another filter.

The honey is spun to remove beeswax.

Transport and storage

Drums of honey are unloaded by forklift. Honey is moved about the factory through stainless steel pipes and, once bottled, along **conveyor belts**.

Packaging the honey

Honey is poured into large metal drums or plastic buckets for bulk sale. Honey to be sold in stores is pumped to special filling machines that fill jars and bottles. A capping machine places and tightens lids. Labels are glued to containers by another machine. Containers are then packed into cartons and stacked onto **pallets**.

A capping machine places and tightens the lids.

Filling machines are programmed by computer to fill each jar or plastic container to the right level.

Processing and packaging workers
Food technologists
Engineers
Production-line workers
Honey tasters
Graphic designers
Transport workers

Cartons of bottles are transported by truck to stores. Bulk containers may be transported to other food **manufacturers** or to ports for shipping overseas.

Honey can be sold locally or exported to other countries. Honey companies use advertising to encourage consumers to buy their product.

Workers from honey companies, called merchandisers, visit stores to make sure that they are receiving the kinds and amounts of honey they need. Merchandisers also organize special displays and tastings to help advertise their company's products.

Large honey companies can afford to advertise their products to a larger audience. They might place ads in magazines or on television. Some companies have their own websites to tell consumers about their products.

Honey is sometimes advertised as an energy food.

Marketing and sales workers

Merchandisers

Shelf-fillers

Checkout operators

Shop assistants

Graphic designers

Copywriters

Film-makers

Actors

Honey can be bought in different kinds of packaging to suit different consumers. For example, bulk honey for export might be packed in large steel drums, smaller drums or large plastic buckets. Bulk packaging is also used to ship honey to other food manufacturers. This honey might be used to make products such as breads, smallgoods, cookies, cakes, drinks, salad dressings, ice cream and breakfast cereals.

People can choose from different kinds of honey in their local supermarkets and stores.

Honey for sale in stores is packed in many different containers, such as small and large glass jars, and twist-and-squeeze plastic bottles.

Honey can bought at markets.

Honey can be used to bake cakes, to flavor savory dishes, to sweeten tea and other drinks, or just spread on fresh bread to make a delicious sandwich.

Home storage

Honey should be stored away from the light, at room temperature. Most liquid honeys will crystallize at low temperatures. It can be gently warmed in hot water to become liquid again. Honey will keep indefinitely in an airtight container.

Honey around the world

In Scandinavian countries such as Denmark, spiced honey cakes are made into gingerbread houses at Christmas time.

In Belgium, some people eat muesli made with honey for breakfast or they add honey to their cereal for taste.

Lavender honey comes from France. French pastry cooks have been making pain d'espice, a spice-bread using honey and spices, for more than 900 years.

In Lebanon and other Middle Eastern countries, people make baklava and many other sweets with honey such as knaffeh, made from vermicelli noodles and honey.

The Chinese often use honey when cooking meats. The dish Peking Duck is coated with honey. Cha shao, or barbecued pork, is also marinated in honey and other ingredients.

The United States produces a great deal of honey. Some people like eating honey on pancakes, muffins or biscuits.

Australia is one of the largest exporters of honey. Australian honeys are very popular because the bees gather nectar from plants that do not grow in other places. Honeys from native eucalypt trees such as yellow box, leatherwood and iron bark only come from Australia.

Make your own honey cake

Use this recipe to make a delicious honey cake at home with help from an adult.

Honey cake

Ingredients

- 1 cup plus 2 tablespoons of butter at room temperature
- $\frac{3}{4}$ cup of honey
- 2 teaspoons of ground ginger
- 2 teaspoons of vanilla essence
- 3 eggs
- 3 teaspoons of baking powder
- $\frac{3}{4}$ cup of plain flour
- $\frac{1}{4}$ cup of milk
- a little extra honey

Equipment

- mixing bowl
- electric mixer or wooden spoon
- 8 inch x 8 inch baking tin, greased with butter and lined with parchment paper
- pastry brush
- skewer
- wire rack
- knife
- spoon

Method

1. Preheat the oven to 350 degrees Fahrenheit.
2. Cut the butter into cubes. Place in a bowl and add the honey. Beat with an electric mixer or wooden spoon until creamy.
3. Mix in the ginger and vanilla.
4. Beat in the eggs one at a time.
5. Mix the baking powder in with the flour. Then gently mix half the flour into the mixture. Add half the milk. Then add the rest of the flour and the rest of the milk.
6. Spoon the mixture into the greased tin and place it in the oven for 35 to 40 minutes. Test that the cake is cooked by inserting a skewer into the center of the cake. If it comes out clean the cake is ready.
7. Let the cake stand for five minutes before turning onto a wire rack.
8. Brush the top of the cake with the extra honey and allow it to cool.

Glossary

bellows bags that are squeezed to blow out air

castes groups of bees that play a different role in the colony

colony group of bees living together

consumer person who buys goods or services

conveyor belts endless strips of material, such as rubber, on rollers used to move something

crystallized when tiny crystals have formed in liquid

embalm preserve a dead body

enzymes substances that cause a chemical change

ferment to cause a chemical reaction that changes the nature of the food

food technologists workers who scientifically test or treat food

honey packers people who process and package honey

larvae young bee grubs

manufacturers people or companies that make goods

Middle Ages period in Europe from 500 A.D. to 1500 A.D.

Middle East area around eastern Mediterranean Sea, from Turkey to North Africa

nectar sugary substance produced by flowers

pallets wooden trays

pollen powdery substance from a flower

preservatives ingredients to keep food fresh

proboscis long mouth part

processing treating in a special way

races groups of the same kind of animal

ripen when enzymes in the worker bees' mouths change nectar sugars into honey sugars

social living together and helping each other

supers boxes that make up a beehive

temperate not too hot and not too cold

Index